Chi's

Sweet Adventures

Created by Konami Kanata
Adapted by Kinoko Natsume

VERTICAL
COMICS

Chi's Sweet Adventures ①

contents

Chi Goes Home, Part 1

MYAA

IT'S DADDY!

OH, CHI YOU'RE AWAKE?

MAMA...

NYAA

MYAA

MOMMY!

MYAA

AH, YOU'RE DONE WITH YOUR AFTERNOON NAP?

MAMA...

MYAA

BUT THAT "VOICE" WAS...

SKAMPER

MYA!!

CHI!

YOHEY!!

MYA MYAA

CHI, LET'S PLAY!!

YAAWN

SOMEONE CALLED CHI?

Continued in Part 2

3

Chi Goes Home, Part 2

MYAA!!
IT WAS YUMMY!

I HAD ANOTHER WEIRD DWEAM...
HAZYO
MYA
HAZY
CHI, ARE YOU AWAKE?

HAA...
I'M STUFFED...

WHAT WAS IT AGAIN?
MYAA?
CHI, WHAT IS IT?

HUH?
DID I FOWGET SOMETHING?

MYAA MYAA MYAA
ARE YOU HUNGRY?

SLUMP
CHI IS ALL STRETCHED OUT.
Ah ha ha
OH WELL...

CHI, HERE'S MILK.
MYAAAN
YAY! IT'S MI-ULK!

Continued in Part 3

Chi Goes Home, Part 3

THAT'S THE KWIK KWAK THING!

GRIN

KLIK KLIK

THIS IS ENOUGH FOR FOOD PREP...

MOMMY, WHAT'RE YOU DOING?

MYA

MYA MYAA ♪

SKITTER

HELPING HELPING! ♪

GCHAK

GCHIK

GCHAK

CHI WILL HELP!

NO, NO!! IT'S DAN-GER-OUS!

MYA!!

HOP HOP

30 minutes later

WELL, TIME TO START WORK AGAIN SOON.

WHA?!

STAY OVER HERE LIKE A GOOD KITTY.

NMRRR...

SKOOTCH

MOMMY IS KEEPING THE FUN TO HER-SELF.

THMP THMP

All the quotes I was still entering disappeared!

MYAA?

CHI CAN DO A GOOD JOB WHEN SHE TWIES!!

FINE, CHI WILL HELP DADDY!

MYAA

Continued in Part 4

5

Chi Goes Home, Part 4

YAY, BOING BOINGS!

BOINNG

BOINNG

OH DEAR...

THIS IS SUPER FUN!

BOINNG

MEOW

YOHEY, LET'S PLAY!

AH, CHI?!

HUH?! MY GOLD ONE IS GONE!

IT'S NO-WHERE!

AAH, MY SUPER-BALL!

BOOO-ING

BOOO-ING

WOOW!!

THAT ONE WAS IMPORT-ANT TO ME! IT'S CHI'S FAULT!!

GO AWAY!!

YOHEY!! DO MORE OF THE BOING THING!!

MYAA MYAAA!

NO, YOU CAN'T, THE GOLD ONE IS MY FAVE!

HMF!

TURN

WHY'RE YOU SO MAD, YOHEY?

Continued in Part 5

FUMYA

A CHANCE!!

WAK

WAH!!

Chi Goes Home, Part 5

YOHEY WAS ANGWY FOR SOME WEASON EVEN THOUGH IT WAS FUN. I WONDER WHY?

GO AWAY!!

MYAA!

YOU PROBABLY DID SOMETHING THE HUMAN DIDN'T LIKE. HUMANS AND CATS ARE DIFFERENT, AFTER ALL.

MRRG.

HUMAN?

CAT?

WASSAT??

MYA?

...NEVER MIND. IT'S GETTING LATE, SO LET'S GO HOME SOON.

CHI'S NOT GOING HOME!

MYA!!

MRGH.

CHI'S NEVER GOING HOME!!

IT'S CHI'S FAULT!!

GO AWAY!!

THAT ONE WAS IMPORTANT TO ME!

I SEE. WELL, I'M GOING HOME TO EAT.

NRR...

FOOD!!

CHI'S GOING HOME!!

MYA!!

BYE BYE!

MYAAN

THAT KID ALWAYS SEEMS SO HAPPY...

Continued in Part 6

7

Chi Goes Home, Part 6

I'M HOME!!

MYA!!

RUSTL

FOOD!!

HUH? HUUUUSSHH

IT'S SO DARK.

MYAAA!!

WHERE IS EVEWY-ONE?!

DADDY! MOMMY! YOHEY!!

MYA MYAA!!

CHI...

MYA?!

POP

CONGRATS!

See?

WHOA!! AMAZING!

MYAA!

WE MADE A FEAST TO CELEBRATE ONE MONTH SINCE CHI CAME HERE.

I MADE AN ALBUM, TOO! IT'S CALLED CHI'S SWEET HOME!

HEH HEH, YOU CAN EAT ALL OF IT!

YUMMY!!

MEWNCH MEWNCH

THIS ONE BRINGS BACK MEM-ORIES, RIGHT?

ISN'T THIS PAGE AMAZING?! I FILLED IT UP WITH PICS OF CHI SLEEPING...

MYA...

I'M STUFFED. CAN'T EAT ANYMORE...

HAA...

MYA?

RUB RUB

WHY'RE YOU CWYING DADDY?

Continued in Part 7

8

Chi Goes Home, Part 7

WHY DON'T YOU FORGIVE HER ALREADY?

MYA

BUT CHI MADE ME LOSE MY SUPER-BALL ...!!

CHI DIDN'T MEAN TO DO ANYTHING BAD.

MYAAN

YOHEY! ♡

B- BUT ...

YOHEY! ♡ ♡

MYAAN ♡

... OKAY.

SQUEEZE

WE'LL MAKE UP.

MYA

MYA!!

HUH?

OH, THERE IT IS!

CHI, LET'S PLAY!

MYAA!!

The End

9

Chi is Stopped, Part 1

Continued in Part 2

10

Chi is Stopped, Part 2

OH WELL, GUESS I'LL JUST HAVE TO CLEAN UP THE CRUMBS.

MYA MYA

VROOOOM

IT WAS SUPER BIG!

WE'RE HOME!

I WONDER IF CHI WAS LONELY.

NO, CHI!!

CHI ATE A WHOLE BUNCH! ISN'T CHI AMAZING?!

MYAAAN!

WHAT THE HECK IS THIS?!

CHI?

MESSY

YOU'RE GETTING IN THE WAY, SO GO OVER THERE!

TOSS

AH! YOHEY! MOMMY!

STUFFED

MYA

WHY?

MYA...

BUT CHI WAS AMAZING...

Continued in Part 3

CHI ATE LOTS OF YUMMY FOOD!

MYAA

...UHH...

Chi is Stopped, Part 3

WE DID IT!

IT'S NICE, I WANTED TO PUT IT DOWN RIGHT HERE.

WE HAVE TO MAKE SURE TO KEEP THE NEW RUG CLEAN.

I'M HOME!

MYAA

CHI! YOU'RE BACK!

FOOD!

MYA

AH !!

STIP

STIP

CHI'S FEET ARE DIRTY !!

YOHEI, BRING A CLOTH !

OKAY!

CHI! NO! STOP !!

MYA ?

WHAT'S WRONG, MOMMY ?

OH, THAT'S RIGHT!!

AAH ...

MYAAN

MOMMY, I'M HOME!

STIP

STIP

Continued in Part 4

Chi is Stopped, Part 4

AH!! A DEAD END!

MYA!

-LOOOM

WAIT! CHI, LEMME CLEAN YOUR FEET!!

YAY! THIS IS SO FUN!!

MYA!

THMP

THMP

SKOOOOT

HUP!!

JUMP!!

MYAA!

YAAH

OH, YOU'RE QUITE LIVELY.

YAAH

AHH!! THE LAUNDRY BASKET ...!

FWUMP

DADDY, PLAYING CHASE IS FUN!

MYAAAN!!

SPRING

DAD, NOW YOUR SHIRTS ARE ALL MUDDY.

AAH, THIS WAS SO FUN...

MYAN

S-SO CUTE ...

HA HA HA, CHI'S SO CUTE AND FULL OF ENERGY.

Hey!

DAD, HELP ME CATCH CHI!!

Continued in Part 5

Chi is Stopped, Part 5

Continued in Part 6

14

Chi is Stopped, Part 6

I WONDER IF CHI WILL BE OKAY IF SHE EATS POTHOS...

HRRM!!

MOMMY KEEPS ALL THE FUN THINGS TO HERSELF...

SWSH

SWSH

TIP TIP

POTHOS IS BAD FOR CATS!

WHAT?!

Toxic for Cats

inf... skin an...

WHOA!

FWISH

CHI! NO NO NO, STOP!!

MYA?!

PLUCK

SWAP

SWAP

MYAAN!!

THIS IS FUN!

MOMMY!!

Whew, that was close...

YOU'RE TOO GWEEDY!!

MYA!!

AAH!!

CHI?!

THIS IS SO NICE!!

TATTERS!

MYA

Continued in Part 7

15

Chi is Stopped, Part 7

CHI, WHAT'RE YOU DOING?

LET'S CLEAR AWAY THE THINGS THAT ARE DANGEROUS FOR CHI!!

SHFF

SWOOP

AAH!!

MOM, DAD!!

IT'S ALL GONE.

ALONE

HUH? WHAT?!

IT'S CHI!

I WONDER IF

ANY OF CHI'S STUFF IS HERE?

GLANCE

IT'S KIND OF ANNOYING, BUT IT'S NOT DANGEROUS FOR HER ...

GLARE

MYA!

THIS IS CHI'S.

WE CAN LET HER PLAY WITH IT.

The End

OH!!

MYA!!

16

Chi Has Lessons, Part 1

AHH, SO SLEEPY...

MYA...

MYAA!

THIS FOOD IS YUMMY!

MRRRM!!

JOLT

MYA?!

DID YOU FORGET OUR PROMISE?!

CHI'S LATE...

YOU ATE A LOT!

MYA!

AH! OUR PWOMISE!! OH, WIGHT!

NRR-RGH.

OKAY, LET'S GET GOING!

MYAA

CHI'S SO FULL...

PWOMISE WITH... BLACKIE... ZZZ...

DON'T FALL ASLEEP!!

MRRRGH!!

Continued in Part 2

MRRRGH...

IRK IRK IRK IRK IRK

THAT DARN CHI...

RUSTL

Chi Has Lessons, Part 2

Continued in Part 3

Chi Has Lessons, Part 3

HOW'S THIS? HISSSS

MORE! MAKE IT INTENSE!

MRRRGH!!

LESSON 1 IS, "HISS!!"

MRR

LESSON 1

"HISS" IS TO MENACE.

LIKE THIS? HISSSSSS!! DUN

HMMM.

NRRN...

DUN

NRGH

BADUM BADUM

WATCH THIS. HERE COMES A DOG.

PANT PANT

HISSSSS!!

JOLT

WUFF?!

ARF ARF ARF !!

JOLT ♪

MYA?!

EEK!!

WHOA!

THIS IS "HISS." YOU TRY IT.

MRR! HMF

OH, DEAR...

WHINE WHINE

WAIT, LOVE

WHY...

DASH

CHI, "HISS" MIGHT NOT BE RIGHT FOR YOU.

Continued in Part 4

19

Chi Has Lessons, Part 4

LESSON 2 IS "HIDE'N'SEEK"!!

LESSON 2

WHEN YOU'RE IN A PINCH, HIDE UNTIL IT PASSES!!

NRR!

MRR! RUSTL

HUH?!

IT'S NOT JUST REGULAR "HIDE'N'SEEK"!! YOU'VE GOT TO JUMP RIGHT IN!!

HOW'S THAT?! I DISAPPEARED AT A MOMENT'S NOTICE, RIGHT?

MRRGH!

RUSTL

WOW!! CHI WANTS TO TRY, TOO!!

MYAAA!!

HUP!!

DASH

MRRRGH!!

OBVIOUSLY WE'LL BUMP INTO EACH OTHER IF WE HIDE IN THE SAME PLACE!!

RUSTL

RUSTL

MYAAN...

BUT...

GEEZ...

LICK

MEEP!!

LOVE, WE'RE GOING.

SHIVER

FMYAA!

RUFF RUFF

...WHAT'S WRONG?

Continued in Part 5

20

Chi Has Lessons, Part 5

LESSON 3 IS THE "HIGH JUMP"!!

MRR

LESSON 3

CAT JUMP

YOU CAN DO THIS EVEN IF YOU'RE NOT GOOD AT "HISS" OR "HIDE 'N' SEEK."

IF YOU JUMP UP TO A HIGH SPOT, THEY CAN'T REACH YOU.

...

SKRAAAPE

...

JUMP UP LIKE THIS.

NRR

SPROING

WHOA!

MYAN!

ARE YOU REALLY A CAT?

MRRM ...

HUPP!

MYAA

MYA?

WHAT'S A CAT?

NEVER MIND, IT'S FINE.

NRR ...

Continued in Part 6

21

Chi Has Lessons, Part 6

IS CHI BAD? CHI CAN'T DO ANYTHING?

MYA...

YOUR "HISS"

HISS

DON'T WORRY.

EVERYONE IS LIKE THIS WHEN THEY FIRST START OUT. LET'S DO LESSONS TOMORROW, TOO.

AND "HIDE'N'SEEK"

WEALLY?! WILL CHI BE ABLE TO DO THE "HISS" AND "JUMP" SOMEDAY?

YEAH, YOU'LL LEARN QUICKLY.

AND "JUMP"

YAY!! CHI WILL DO HER BEST!

MYAA

M-MRR...

THAT'S A BIGGER JUMP THAN EARLIER...

ARE ALL BAD.

MRR

...

Continued in Part 7

22

Chi Has Lessons, Part 7

I KNEW IT.

SNOOO

THIS IS YUMMY!!

MYAA ♡

MRRARR!!

CHI!! AGAIN?! YOU FORGOT AGAIN?!

JOLT

MYA?!

CHI'S LATE... WAIT, DON'T TELL ME SHE...

...

OH, BLACKIE!!

WE'RE GOING!!

MRRR

CHI, YOU ATE LOTS TODAY, TOO.

I'M STUFFED. ♡

MYAA

SLUMP

HUH...? CHI FOWGOT SOMETHING...? ZZZ...

WAKE UP!!

MRRARR!!

THIS IS... DEJA VU...?!

The End

Chi Has Cheese, Part 1

NO MORE FOR YOU!

MORE! GIVE CHI SOME MORE!

MYA MYA

WE'RE HAVING PANCAKES FOR BREAKFAST!

YAY! I'M DIGGING IN!

STEAM STEAM

STEAM

STEAM

OOOH, WHAT'S THIS GOOD-SMELLING THING?

MYA?

MELT MELT MELT

WELL, THEN I'M EATING MY... HUH?!

BAM

CHI, YOU WANT SOME, TOO? YOU CAN HAVE JUST A BITE!

YAY!

NYOM NYOM

I DIDN'T EVEN GET A SINGLE BITE!!

No way...

WAAARM

SOOOOOFT Y-YUMMY!

AND WARM

Continued in Part 2

Chi Has Cheese, Part 2

THERE, THERE.
PET
PET
HAAAH.

WHERE IS IT...? GLANCE GLANCE CHI'S LOOKING FOR YUMMY FOOD!!

PREET
OH, IT FINALLY BOILED.
DADDY, WHAT ABOUT THE YUMMY THING?!
MYA

AH, IT'S DADDY!!
OH, CHI, YOU'RE CUTE TODAY, TOO!
MYA!

TIME TO BRING THIS ON THE SCENE!! THIS JAMAICAN BLUE MOUNTAIN COFFEE!!
WAS-SAT? IS IT YUM-MY?!
MYAA!

MYAAN RUB RUB
DADDY, DO YOU HAVE ANYTHING YUMMY?

HM? WHAT IS IT, CHI? YOU WANT SO MUCH ATTENTION TODAY.
Ha ha ha
MYAAA!
THAT'S NOT WHAT CHI WANTS!!
PET
PET

WHAT IS IT CHI? YOU WANT ATTEN-TION?
MYA!
DADDY, WHAT ARE YOU GIVING ME?!

Continued in Part 3

25

Chi Has Cheese, Part 3

IT SMELLS WEIRD, BUT...

CHI'S DWINKING IT!

MYAA

So fragrant!!

AAH, DELI-CIOUS.

LICK

OOO

CHI, WANT SOME? HEH, JUST KIDDING.

WASSAT? SMELLS WEIRD.

SNIFF ? SNIFF

BLECH!

YUCKY!

COME TO THINK OF IT, WHERE'D I PUT THAT FILE...?

TUNK

DADDY'S FOOD TASTES STWANGE!!

CHI, WHAT'S WRONG?

MIII!

SKITTER SKITTER

HUH? I CAN'T FIND IT, WEIRD.

A CHANCE!!

MYA ♪

KAKLE

Continued in Part 4

Chi Has Cheese, Part 4

CHI'S NOT GIVING UP!!

RISE

OH! THAT'S MOMMY'S PWEY!

HOW'S THIS?!

GRAH

MYA!

LEAP

BAM

MYAA!!

SMIRK

CHI KNOWS MOMMY'S PWEY IS YUMMY!!

CH... CHI DID IT.

HUFF

HUFF

HUFF

MYA ...!!

HUP!

BAM

MYAA

JUUUMP!

MYAA ♪

PWEY!!

HUH?! I CAN'T WEACH AT ALL.

FMYA

SPLAT

Continued in Part 5

27

Chi Has Cheese, Part 5

THIS ONE NEXT!

MYA!!

I WONDER WHAT PWEY MOMMY HAS?

RUSTL

AAANG!

CHI'S DIGGING IN!

WHAT'S THIS? IS IT YUMMY?

CHI'S DIGGING IN!

M—MY MOUF...

MYA MYA GAH...

CHOMP

....

...CHI'S FOOD WEALLY IS THE BEST.

BLEH! IT'S TOUGH AND TASTES WEIRD!!

PEH

Continued in Part 6

28

Chi Has Cheese, Part 6

WASSAT?

YAY

YAY

DOING CHEESE FONDUE FOR DINNER SURE IS FUN.

MY FOLKS SENT US TONS OF CHEESE!

HOW DO WE EAT THIS?

OH RIGHT, THIS IS YOUR FIRST FONDUE, YOHEI.

YOU DIP FOOD INTO THE CHEESE LIKE SO...

OOH!

AND THEN TAKE IT OUT LIKE THIS!

STREETCH

WHOOA!!

I WANNA TRY, TOO!

OKAY, THEN USE THIS SKEWER.

YAY!

MYAA!

PUT IT IN THE CHEESE...

CHI AND YOHEI ARE GAGA ABOUT IT!

Myaa

Yay

STRETCH

CHI'S STRETCHING AS MUCH AS THE CHEESE!

Continued in Part 7

Chi Has Cheese, Part 7

CHI, YOU OKAY ?!

HOT HOT HOT HOT !!

MYAMYA!!

Yummy!

MYAAAN

CHI WANTS TO EAT THE STWETCHY THING!

NOM

I'LL TRY BREAD NEXT.

STRETCH

Y... Y... SOFT !

YUMMY!!

WARM !!

NOW'S MY CHANCE!!

WHOA, IT'S SO LONG!

MYAA

I'M FULL! ♡

CHI'S SUCH A GLUTTON !

The End

HUH ?

MYAA

CHI TOTALLY CAUGHT THE STRETCHY THING!!

Chi Does Halloween, Part 1

HUH?

GIVE CHI SOME!

MYA!!

TRICK OR

TREAT!

CHI, DID YOU GET A SHOCK FROM STRANGERS VISITING?

MYA!

PWEY!!

IF YOU DON'T GIVE US CANDY, WE'LL GIVE YOU MISCHIEF!

YOU'RE ALL SO CUTE! I'LL GIVE YOU SOME CANDY!

MYA!

SMELLS YUMMY!

THERE'S NOTHING TO WORRY ABOUT...

WHERE'RE WE GOING? WHERE'S THE PWEY?!

MYAA!

HERE YOU GO!

MYA!

THANKS, MA'AM!

THERE, THERE...

MYAA!

PWEY!

Continued in Part 2

Bye bye!

COME BY AGAIN!

MYAAN!

MOMMY, GIVE CHI SOME PWEY, TOO!

Chi Does Halloween, Part 2

CHI, YOU LIKE MY CAPE?

Hey, I can't walk...

THIS IS FUN!

MYAA!

WE'RE BACK!

TRICK OR TREAT!!

THIS IS NICE!

MYA MYA

Ah ha ha...

CHI, TODAY WE DRESS UP AND GET CANDY!

IT LOOKS GOOD ON YOU. DID SOMEONE BUY IT FOR YOU?

YEAH! I'M A WIZARD!

WAS-SAT?! IT'S FLUT-TERY!

MYA?!

CHI, YOU LISTEN-ING?

SWIPE

MYAA!!

SHUDDUP!! CHI'S PLAYING NOW!

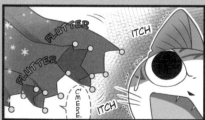

FLUTTER

FLUTTER

FLUTTER

C'MERE.

ITCH

ITCH

CHI...

DADDY'S TWYING TO GET CHI'S PWEY!!

MYA!

Continued in Part 3

OH?

HUH?

BAM

Chi Does Halloween, Part 3

Continued in Part 4

Chi Does Halloween, Part 4

CHI, WAIT! JUST ONE PICTURE...!!

ESCAPE!!

MYAAAAAA!!

A-aaah!

SKEDADDLE

DON'T CATS HATE WEARING CLOTHES ...?

AW, YOU THINK? SHE'LL BE FINE FOR JUST A LITTLE WHILE.

Right, Chi?

MYA?

I GOT HER!

LEMME GO!!

GOOD JOB, YOHEI!! HERE WE GO!

FLAIL

FLAIL

MYAA!!

I'LL HOLD HER GENTLY LIKE THIS SO SHE DOESN'T STRUGGLE ...

??

MRARN!!

FLASH

AH!

PUT ON THE HOOD ...

AND JUST DO THIS BUTTON ...

YANK

MYAA ...

IT HAS A LITTLE TOO MUCH MOVEMENT ...

Continued in Part 5

OOH, HOW CUTE!! SHE'S A BUNNY KITTY!

T-TOO TIGHT ...

I'LL BRING THE CAMERA NOW! JUST KEEP HER LIKE THAT!!

MYA ...

Chi Does Halloween, Part 5

LOOK, CHI, IT'S FUN!

SWRRRR

MYA?!

SHE DOESN'T LIKE THE BUNNY OUTFIT BECAUSE IT'S TIGHT! IF IT WAS A CAPE, SHE'D LIKE IT!

LET'S MAKE A CAPE!

SHE CAME OUT.

MYAA!!

GOTTA DO IT NOW...

SWRRR

SNEAK

CREEP

OKAY, YOHEI! GO MEASURE CHI!

OKAY!!

YAAAAH!!

DADDY'S TWYING TO DO WEIRD THINGS TO CHI AGAIN!!

SLASH

OUCH!!

CHI'S CWANKY AND NOT COMING OUT!

CHI...

...

I GUESS WE CAN'T FORCE HER TO GO ALONG WITH HUMAN WHIMS.

BOO hoo...

SNUB

CHI DOES NOT LIKE DADDY.

Continued in Part 6

...

I CAN'T MEASURE HER LIKE THIS... OH, I KNOW!

36

Chi Does Halloween, Part 6

HUH? WASSAT?

MYA?

WHAT'S THIS?!

ROLL

IT'S SUPER FUN!

ROLL

MOM, DAD, LOOK!

OH!

CHI IS SO GREAT!

MYA?

WHAT?

SHE DRESSED HERSELF UP!

HERE'S CANDY FOR THE CUTE MUMMY!

YAY! CHI'S PWEY!

MYAAN!♡

FLASH

CHI, THANKS FOR DOING THIS FOR ME!!

Yum~!

FLASH

SO CUTE!!

BUT TODAY WAS HOWWIBLE...

GLANCE...

I GOT A GREAT SHOT!

GUESS IT'S OKAY BECAUSE

THIS IS YUMMY!

MYAA

Continued in Part 7

37

Chi Does Halloween, Part 7

MOMMY, YOU LISTENING?!

MYAA?!

The next day

THE CWISPY PWEY WAS YUMMY.

WHAT IS IT, CHI? YOU WANT TO PLAY?

MYA!

CWISPY PWEY!!

MOMMY, GIMME THE CWISPY PWEY!

MYAN!

THEN LET'S GO FIND DAD AND YOHEI.

CWISPIES!!

MYAAAN!!

CHI WANTS THE CWISPIES!

MYA

ROLL ROLL

THERE THERE,

MYAAA!!

PWEY!!

MRMM.

MYA...

The End

38

Chi Gets Brushed, Part 1

MYAA

THIS IS FOR YOU, KENTO.

TIP TIP TIP

WELL, CHI STILL NEEDS DINNER, SO WHY DON'T YOU GIVE IT TO HER?

YES!! I WILL FEED HER!!

ON IT!!

YES, YES, DINNER FOR CHI, TOO.

STARE

...

MYAAAN

CHI, HERE, IT'S DINNER!

MYAA?!

HUH?! DADDY'S GIVING ME FOOD TODAY?!

I WISH CHI WOULD FOLLOW ME AROUND LIKE SHE DOES TO YOU, MIWA.

HUH?

OOHH!! CHI!!

MYAAAAN!

HUWWY UP WITH THE FOOD!!

RUB

sigh

BUT GETTING FOLLOWED AROUND IS A BOTHER, YOU KNOW.

I WISH I COULD SAY THAT JUST ONCE.

MYAA

RUB

Awww, Chi likes me!!

HAPPY!

MYAA!

HUWWY UP!

DAD'S KINDA SIMPLE.

WHISPER

YEAH.

Continued in Part 2

Chi Gets Brushed, Part 2

GIVE BACK CHI'S FLAPPY THING!!

MYAN!

NO, CHI, YOU'RE IN THE WAY!

YAY! A FLAPPY THING!

IT'S SO FUN!

MYAA?!

HUH?! IT GOT SUCKED UP!!

SLKK

VROO

MYA?!

SORRY, CHI, I'M GOING IN FRONT OF YOU.

VRRROOM

MYAA!!

VRROOM

WAIT, WILL CHI GET...

HUH?!

IT'S GONE!!

...CHI IS DONE PLAYING FOR THE DAY!

?

VROOM

HAZY

Continued in Part 3

WHERE'D YOU HIDE THE FLAPPY THING?!

VROO

Chi Gets Brushed, Part 3

WAAH, CHI'S GONNA GET EATEN!!

VRMMM

VROOO

SNOO...

VROOO

OH, GOOD, IT WAS JUST A DWEAM.

MYA?!

Haah...

THIS IS SO FUN!

SORRY, CHI. YOU'RE IN THE WAY THERE, TOO. CAN YOU MOVE?

VROOO

CHI'S SLEEPING HERE!!

MYAA!!

VROOO

HUH?!

AH!

LAY DOWN HERE.

MRRR

MYAA

VR RR RR RR RR

MYAAA?!

WH-WHAT'S THAT?!

Continued in Part 4

Chi Gets Brushed, Part 4

LET ME GO !!

MYAAAA !!

CHI, LOOK, IT'S JUST A BRUSH!! IT'S NOT THAT SCARY!!

FLAIL

FLAIL

MAKE SURE TO BRUSH CHI!!

We're off!

WELL, THAT'S WHAT THEY SAID.

BRUSH

BRUSH

...HUH?

MYA?

THIS IS FOR YOUR SAKE, CHI...!!

WHAT?! I'VE GOT A BAD FEELING !!

MYA ?!

Mwa ha ha...

BWUSH BWUSH.

OH, YOU'VE SUDDENLY CALMED DOWN.

I WEMEMBER THIS...

MYA !!

ESCAPE!!

CATCH

FLUFFY...

AND WARM...

WHAT WAS IT...

Continued in Part 5

FORGIVE ME, CHI!!

MYAA !!

WHAT'RE YOU DOING!!

42

Chi Gets Brushed, Part 5

CHI...

MYA?

DAD NEEDS TO DO SOME WORK, SO THAT'S ALL FOR NOW.

SHOOP

MYAAN ♡

GOOD KITTY.

WELL, BACK TO WORK!!

MYAAA!!

MORE!! MORE BWUSH BWUSH!!

AAHH.♡

MYAAA ♡

MRAOOWN

BWUSH BWUSH!!

Ha ha ha

WOW! CHI LOVES IT!

LOOKS LIKE BRUSHING WENT WELL.

AARGH!! I'M GONNA FINISH UP WORK REALLY FAST

RROO

AAAR

SO I CAN GO BACK TO HANG-ING OUT WITH CHI!!

KCHAK

KCHAK

Continued in Part 6

OH, IT'S ALREADY SO LATE?

Chi Gets Brushed, Part 6

VROOOM

WHAT'RE YOU DOING?!

RAWR

MYAAAAA!!

I WANT TO VACUUM THE SOFA, SO WILL YOU MOVE FOR ME?

SORRY, CHI.

VROOO

IF YOU DON'T LIKE IT, MOVE!

HUH...? TH-THIS IS:...

MYA ...?

CHI'S NOT MOVING ANY-MORE...

CHI STAYS HERE.

THIS IS NICE!

MYAAA

VROOO

HUH?!

VRROOOM

OKAY ...

CHI'S IGNOWING IT.

...

HAHAAN!

MYAA

VRRROOM

NO WAY!!

Continued in Part 7

IF YOU REFUSE TO MOVE,

Mwhahaa...

THEN I HAVE TO RESORT TO FORCE.

Chi Gets Brushed, Part 7

GLANCE

...

CHI
...?

whew

I'M DOOONE~!!

CHI LIKES THIS ONE BETTER.

MYAA ♡

HUH?!

CHI, SORRY FOR... HUH?

HAAAAA AAA AA

VROOOM

GEEZ. CAN'T BE HELPED.

MYAAↄ

VRRROOM

APPARENTLY CHI LIKES BEING VACUUMED.

MYAA

HAHAAN.

WHAT'S WRONG DADDY? THIS IS SUPER FUN!

VROOOM

MYAAA

CHI
...

VROOOOM

LOOK!!

CHI, IT'S YOUR FAVORITE BRUSH!

The End

45

Chi Goes Camping, Part 1

LET CHI OUTTA HERE!!

MYA MYAAA!!

FLAIL FLAIL

MYA MYAA!!

CHI DOESN'T LIKE THIS CAGE...

MYA??

LET...

MYA??

MYA MYAAA!!

LEMME OUT!!

AH, WHAT'S WRONG, CHI?

I WONDERED WHY SHE GOT SO QUIET...

KNEW IT.

heh heh

SHE MUST BE BOUNCING WITH EXCITEMENT TO GO OUT WITH US!

MYA!!

MYA!

I SEE.

SHE'S SOUND ASLEEP.

HEE HEE, I WONDER IF SHE'S DREAMING OF FOOD.

Continued in Part 2

Chi Goes Camping, Part 2

Fuji Treasure Car Camp Site → IN

CHI, WE'RE HERE.

RUSTL

WASSAT?

HUH?!

CHI WAS ASLEEP!!

W-WHOA!

DRIFFT

MYA!!

WHOA! WHAT IS THIS PLACE?!

MYAA?!

SHOOM

OH, FOUND YOU!

MYAA♪

CHI'S GONNA GO EXPLORE!!

AH, CHI, WAIT!

HOP

CHI SURE IS HAVING FUN.

THIS IS SO FUN!

MYAA

SKITTER

48

Continued in Part 3

HUH? WASSAT?

KRUNCH KRUNCH

THERE YOU ARE, CHI.

YOHEY!!

MYA!!

YAY! IT'S CWUNCHIES!

KRUNCH

ROLL

ROLL

KRUNCH

WHAT'RE YOU DOING?

MYA!

KRAK

WHOA! IT CWACKLED!

AAH...

KRUNCH

CWACKLE CWUNCH!

KRAKLE

CHI, LET'S GO BACK TO WHERE EVERYONE IS!

KRUNCH

THERE'S LOTS OF SOUNDS!

KRAKLE

FLUFFY CWUNCHIES.

RUSTL

RUSTL

THIS IS SUPER FUN!

MYAA!

KRUNCH

WHOA, CHI, YOU'RE IN THE WAY.

HOP

KRAKLE

KRUNCH

KRAKLE

Continued in Part 4

Chi Goes Camping, Part 4

50

Continued in Part 5

Chi Goes Camping, Part 5

MYA ? WASSAT?

MYAA!! IT'S WET!! WHIP WHIP WHIP

MYA!! IT'S WIPPLY!!

RIIIPPPLE HUH?!

BLUUURRY THAT WEIRDO FROM BEFORE IS GONE!

SOMETHING'S IN THERE!! SPLISH

COME ON, CHI! MYAA! OH WELL!

Continued in Part 6

Chi Goes Camping, Part 6

YOU PLAYED WITH DRAGON-FLIES,

WOW, ALL YOUR PICTURES CAME OUT GREAT!

ATE SOUR BERRIES FROM A TREE,

HRM ?!

CHI'S SCARED OF SOMETHING HERE!

AND HAD YUMMY ICE CREAM!

IT'S OKAY, DAD. LOOK AT THE NEXT ONE!

WHAT ...?

YOU HAD FUN, RIGHT?

IT WAS FUN!

MYAA

OH, RIGHT, IT WAS A SWAN BOAT.

SEE?

Continued in Part 7

Chi Goes Camping, Part 7

WE'RE GOING TO MAPLE FALLS!

BE CAREFUL ALONG THE WAY!

MYAN

YOHEY, LET'S HUWWY UP AND GET GOING!!

AH, CHI?!

HOP

CHI, IT'S JUST THE TWO OF US ON THIS BIG ADVENTURE!!

YAY! A WALK WITH YOHEY!

MYA♪

YOHEY♡

MYAAA♡

...

CHI, YOU'RE NOT SCARED AT ALL. THAT'S KINDA REASSURING.

MYA!!

STAGGER STAGGER

RUSTL...

IT'S DARKER THAN I THOUGHT...

MYA?

Maple Falls

OKAY, WE'RE OFF

MYAA

ON OUR ADVENTURE!

The End

Chi Adventures, Part 1

54

Continued in Part 2

Chi Adventures, Part 2

LOOK, CHI, THE WATER IS RUSHING BY!!

YUM!

MYAA ♡

THIS WATER TASTES GOOD!! CHI, YOU TRY SOME, TOO!

YOHEY LOOKS LIKE HE LIKES IT!

MYA?

CHI?

...

BUT... MIULK WOULD BE TASTIER...

BURBLE

CHI WILL TRY SOME, TOO...

STARE

MYAAAN

MIULK PLEASE!

SLURP

MIULK!

MYAAA!!

CHI, LET'S GET GOING.

Continued in Part 3

Chi Adventures, Part 3

I WONDER IF WE'RE ALMOST THERE...

MYA ♪

IT'S ALL TWISTY!!

MYA MYA MYA

CHI, THAT'S DANGEROUS!

BAT BAT BAT

!!

RUSTL RUSTL RUSTL

JOLT

I HAVE NO CHOICE ...!!

TAKE THAT!!

WHAK WHAK

RUSTL

WHOA, A SNAKE!!

MYA?!

SLITHER

ZWING

GO AWAY!!

MYA?!

SKFF

W-WHOA! WASSAT?!

MYAA!!

I DID IT! I DEFEATED THE SNAKE! NOW WE'RE SAFE.

MYAA~

WHY? BUT IT LOOKED LIKE FUN!!

Continued in Part 4 ♥

Chi Adventures, Part 4

WHOA... WHAT A LONG STAIRCASE.

MYA!

Maple Falls
Right Ahead

OH WELL, I GUESS I'LL HAVE TO CARRY YOU.

MYA?!

WELL, NO CHOICE BUT TO CLIMB IT.

hup

two

CHI, LET'S DO OUR BEST!

MYAA

BUT... I WONDER HOW FAR UP THESE STAIRS GO.

huff

huff

RIGHT, CHI?!

CHI?!

FWUMP

CHI...?

SNOO

OH, SHE'S SLEEPING.

MYA?!

SLUMP

SO TIRED... CAN'T CLIMB ANYMORE...

ZZZ...

57

Continued in Part 5

Chi Adventures, Part 5

58

Continued in Part 6

Chi Adventures, Part 6

Continued in Part 7

Chi Adventures, Part 7

The End

Chi Competes, Part 1

Mama!
Ah ha ha ha
HUFF HUFF HUFF
YAY!
YAY!

HOW WAS THAT? DID YOU SEE?!
MRAOW!!
HMF

LET'S HAVE ANOTHER MATCH!
BUT IT'LL ALWAYS BE THE SAME RESULT.
KEH, GLANCE

Ahh, I lost again.
But you're still pretty good.

READY, GO!!
DASH

Let's have a match tomorrow, too!
Ah ha ha ha!
What, again?
....

KEH, I'M TOTALLY FASTER!
MRAR!!
DASH DASH

KEH!

Continued in Part 2

MYAA

THIS PLACE LOOKS NICE.

THIS KID'S A SHRIMP AND CAN'T EVEN JUMP. KEH, AN EASY VICTORY!!

UPSIE...

KEH! I'M MAKING THIS MY TURF, SO SCRAM!

JOLT

MRR!!

MYA?!

HAA, CHI MADE IT UP! ...HUH?

YAY! LET'S PLAY TOGETHER!!

MYAA!!

M-MRR...

UH, NO, LISTEN, THIS IS MY...

YOU'RE PRETTY SMALL, HUH!

MYAA

MRAR?!

CHI'S GOING UP THERE!

MYAA

LISTEN TO ME!!

MRAOW!!

I-I GOT CALLED SMALL BY THIS LITTLE BRAT.

HEY, HEY, WHAT DO YOU WANNA PLAY?

MYAAA!

62

Continued in Part 3

Chi Competes, Part 3

63

Continued in Part 4

Chi Competes, Part 4

Continued in Part 5

Chi Competes, Part 5

65

Continued in Part 6

Chi Competes, Part 6

CHI'S HOME!

MYAA

CHI, WELCOME HOME.

WE CHASED PWEY.

MYAA

POMF

MYA

CHI, YOU'RE REALLY CHATTY TODAY.

HERE'S MILK.

YOHEY, DID YOU KNOW? OUTSIDE...

MYAA!!

AND IT WAS WEALLY...

YAAAAWN

MYAA?

LAP

LAP

SNOO...

SHE'S ASLEEP.

THERE WAS A SMALL KID AND...

PWAH

MYA

MYA

WE PLAYED TAG TOGETHER.

IT WAS A LOT OF FUN.

MRMM

The End

Chi Meets a Parakeet, Part 1

WHOA, IT'S SO CUTE!

tweet?!

IT'S PWEY!

WHAT'S HE DOING HERE?

tweet

chirp chirp chirp

NOW, NOW...

RATTLE

RATTLE

chirp

MYAA

MYAA

MYAA

MRS. AKASHI FROM APT. 104 IS ON VACATION,

SO SHE ASKED US TO KEEP HIM WHILE SHE'S AWAY.

GSHAK

THAT WAS CLOSE!

YOU CAN'T EAT HIM, CHI!!

AH!! CHI?!

MYAA

LET'S GO OVER HERE.

PWEY!

MYAA!!

IS THIS A GOOD IDEA...?

FLAIL FLAIL

chirp

Continued in Part 2

Continued in Part 3

Chi Meets a Parakeet, Part 3

69

Continued in Part 4

Chi Meets a Parakeet, Part 4

Continued in Part 5

CHI IS ME!

CHI IS ME!

MYAAA!!

SKITTER SKITTER

MRAAAR!!

CHI IS ME!

CHI IS ME!

MYAAA!

HELP!!

FLAIL

FLAIL

MYAA!!

CHI IS ME!

SWOOSH

CHI IS CHI!

SKITTER SKITTER

WE'RE HOME... WHOA?!

THE PARAKEET ESCAPED HIS CAGE!!

SHAMBLES

CHI IS ME!

FLAP

FLAP

HAAA.

WHEEZ

WHEEZ

MOOOMMY!!

MYAAA!!

CHI, WHAT HAPPENED?

IT'S PWEY!

WE DEFINITELY CAN'T LEAVE CHI HOME ALONE...

IT WAS SCAWY!

MYAAA

71

The End

Chi Goes Out, Part 1

HEY!

COME LOOK AT THIS REAL QUICK!

CHI, LET'S PLAY.

MYA!!

FLIT FLIT

TINKL

TA-DAA

I BOUGHT CHI A COLLAR.

VAAAY!!

MYAA!!

FLIT FLIT

TINKL TINK TINK

I DON'T THINK SHE LIKES IT...

THAT CAN'T BE TRUE! It's too cute!!

TINKL

I CAUGHT IT!!

MYAN!!

TINK TINK TINKL

WHAP

?

SOMETHING'S ON ME...?

TINK TINK TINK

BAT BAT BAT

YAY! THIS IS FUN!

MYAA

Whew

CHI SEEMS TO BE FINE WITH THE COLLAR.

73

Continued in Part 2

Chi Goes Out, Part 2

Continued in Part 3

Chi Goes Out, Part 3

WE'RE HERE,

NRR

IT'S THE PARK!

MYAA

ARE THESE BLACKIE'S FWIENDS?

WELL, SOMETHING LIKE THAT.

NRR

MYA?

HEY, LET'S PLAY!

MYAA!

NRR

WE DON'T PLAY.

CHI'S NEVER BEEN TO THE PARK AT NIGHT!

MYAA!

THERE'S A LOT THAT'S DIFFERENT BETWEEN DAY AND NIGHT.

TINK

TINK

MYA?

WHY NOT?

PASSING THE TIME IN SILENCE LIKE THIS IS WHAT GROWN-UPS DO.

NRR ...

MYAA?

GROWN-UPS?

HUH?

AH!

JUST PIPE DOWN ALREADY.

MRGH

MYAA!?

OKAY...

...

HEY, WHAT'RE YOU GUYS DOING?

MYAA!!

K-KEEP IT DOWN!!

MRGH!!

IT'S GETTING A LITTLE MORE EXCITING!!

MYA!!

I TOLD YOU TO KEEP QUIET!

MRRGH!

Continued in Part 4

BIZNESS IS BORING.

LOOKS LIKE YOU GOT A PEEK INTO THE ADULT WORLD.

MRR

WHAT'S WITH THAT ANNOYING NOISE?!

MRAAR!!

OH, IT'S THE SMALL ONE I PLAYED WITH EARLIER!

MYA!!

MRAR!

DON'T CALL ME SMALL!!

CHI DOESN'T KNOW, BUT IT'S OKAY.

KEH!!

TINK

HEY, WHAT DO YOU WANNA PLAY?

MYA!

TINK

MRAR!

I'M NOT PLAYING, SO DON'T FOLLOW ME!

NOBODY'S HERE.

WE'RE THE ONLY ONES IN THIS PARK RIGHT NOW.

MYA

MRR

HEY...!

TINK TINK TINK TINK

MYAA!

THEN LET'S PLAY!

MRR!

TINK

76

Continued in Part 5

Chi Goes Out, Part 5

The End

Continued in Part 2

Chi Goes to a "Nice Place," Part 2

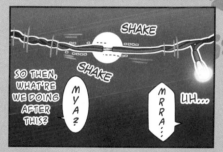

79

Continued in Part 3

Chi Goes to a "Nice Place," Part 3

KEH, WE WERE A LITTLE LATE.

IS THIS THE NICE PLACE?

MYAA?

MRR

HEY, WHAT DO YOU WANNA PLAY NEXT?

I DIDN'T GET TO EAT ANY...

YAY! LET US IN!

DON'T STAND AROUND DOIN' NOTHIN'! LET'S GO!!

AREN'T YOU HUNGRY?

MRRAW

SQUEEZE

SQUEEZE

MRAAR!!

MYAA!

CHI ATE LOTS AT HOME, SO CHI'S OKAY!

MYAA!

MYAA!!

AHH, THAT WAS FUN!

MYAA

EMPTY!

...

COCCHI, WHERE ARE YOU GOING?

DON'T FOLLOW ME...

MYA?

MRR

80

Continued in Part 4

Chi Goes to a "Nice Place,"
Part 4

Continued in Part 5

The End

Chi Goes Back, Part 1

Continued in Part 2

Chi Goes Back, Part 2

OPEN UP!

CHI'S OUTSIDE!

MYAA~

COME TO THINK OF IT, I HAVEN'T SEEN CHI AROUND.

AH!!

YOHEY!! OPEN UP!!

DADDY! CHI'S OVER HERE!!

MYAA

YOHEI, HAVE YOU SEEN CHI?

This hot cocoa is tasty~

MYA...

MAYBE SHE'S BEHIND THE CURTAIN...

SWISH

WHY?!

SLUMP

MYAA~

SHE'S NOT THERE.

MYAAA!!

DADDY!!

Continued in Part 3

Chi Goes Back, Part 3

85

Continued in Part 4

WHAT THE HECK!!

MYAA~!

CHI IS...

CHI WAS OUTSIDE FOR SO LONG!!

IT WAS WEALLY COLD!!

SHE'S ANGRY...

MYAA!!

MYAA!!

IS...

HERE, I'LL BRUSH YOU.

HERE'S SOME MILK.

CHI WAS WORRIED THE WHOLE TIME!!

MYAA~!

FUME FUME

HAAAH!

CHI IS...!! LAP

LAP

BWUSHY BWUSHY!

Continued in Part 5

Chi Goes Back, Part 5

A PRESENT FROM MRS. CLAUS.

CHI'S DIGGING IN!!

NOM

AH!!

FISH CAKES ...

WITH CHI'S FACE!!

YUMMY!!

CHI, REALLY LOOK AT IT!

MNCH

MNCH

They turned out really well.

Wow! Amazing!

Right?

I'M STUFFED ~!

LICK

LICK

CHI DOESN'T UNDERSTAND DRAWINGS ...

WASSAT?

MYA?

LOOK CHI, IT HAS YOUR FACE ON IT.

SHE FELL ASLEEP.

SNOO

MAMA ....

The End

Chi Rings In the New Year

The End

Chi Has a New Year's Feast

WOW! IT'S A FEAST!

HERE YOU GO!!

WHOA 2!

TA-DAAA

MYA? WASSAT?

THANKS FOR THE FEAST!

MEOWNCH

MEOWNCH

GIVE CHI SOME, TOO !!

MYAAA!!

NO, IT'S ALL TOO SALTY FOR YOU.

WAAH

YUMMY!!

WAAH

MYAA~!

HEH HEH HEH... I THOUGHT THIS WOULD HAPPEN,

SO I MADE A FEAST JUST FOR CHI...!!

RUMMAGE RUMMAGE

DO YOU LIKE IT?

SO YUMMY!

MYAA!

The End

KEH, IT'S QUIET.

MRARZ!

PUUUULL

HM? WHAT'S THAT?

LUCKY BAG

WHAT'S THIS FOR...?

DANGLE

I KNOW!!

IT LOOKS LIKE A REALLY SUSPICIOUS BAG...

DUN DUN DUN DUN

IT'S WARM WHEN USED LIKE THIS!!

MRAR!

I'M SUPER SMART!

RUSTL

BUT IF THERE'S FOOD IN IT, IT'D GO TO WASTE, SO I SHOULD CHECK...

AH HA HA! COCCHI, YOU'RE SO WEIRD!

MYAA

SHEDDAP!

MRRRAO!

The End

Chi Plays a Game

UHH, I DUNNO...

HAAH!

AW, C'MON, CHI!

WHAT'RE YOU DOING?

MYAA

Maybe here?

I think that's good!

UH...

OH, MY...

HMM.

WASSAT?

MYA!

SHE FINISHED THE LUCKY FACE!

YAY! CHI WANTS TO PLAY, TOO!

MYAA!

FWIT FWIT FWIT FWIT FWIT

HUH?! CHI!!

CHI'S AMAZING!!

MYA?

91

The End

CHI HATES THE COLD. WHERE IS SOME PLACE WARM?

More chilly kitty days are in store.

SHIVER

SHIVER

Work-disrupting cats may appear!

CHI CAN EVEN SLEEP IN THIS KINDA PLACE. SOOO SLEEPY...

Watch for leaping cats, itchy with curiosity!

WRIGL

CHI'S GONNA CATCH A BIG PWEY!

WRIGL

PLEASE BE KIND TO ALL KINDS OF CHI!

Chi's Sweet Adventures Vol. 2
On Sale Summer 2018!